D0274732

buddhist

peace recipes

We are grateful to The Metropolitan Nikko, New Delhi and Marriott WelcomHotel, New Delhi, for facilitating the photography.

Second impression 2007
This edition © Roli & Janssen BV
Published in India
by
Roli Books in arrangement with Roli & Janssen
M-75 Greater Kailash II (Market), New Delhi 110 048, India
Ph: ++91-11-29212271, 29212782, 29210886; Fax: (011) 29217185
E-mail: roli@vsnl.com, Website: rolibooks.com

ISBN 978-81-7436-312-1

Editor: Neeta Datta
Design: Cumulus

Printed and bound in Singapore

Text: Pushpesh Pant
Photographs: Dheeraj Paul

buddhist

peace recipes

Lustre Press
Roli Books

To the memory of my parents,
Dr Krishna Chandra and Jayanti Pant,
for their gift of 'taste' and 'quest for knowledge'.
And, for my son, Indrajit, in appreciation of his love,
understanding and unflinching support.

Contents

Buddhist Repast

THE 'REALM OF BUDDHIST FOOD' encompasses more than half of humanity. From the land of its birth, India, the gospel spread to Sri Lanka when the children of Emperor Ashoka—Mahendra and Sangmitra—carried it with them. In subsequent centuries the new faith travelled to Burma, Thailand, Cambodia, and Indonesia. Intrepid monks and scholars conveyed the message of the Enlightened One to China via Tibet, wherefrom it reached Mongolia, Japan, and Korea.

In one of his sermons the Buddha compares the human body to a string in the musical instrument, veena—if it is stretched too tight, imposing on it a hard ascetic discipline of self-denial, it may break and if it is allowed to hang loose, following the path of least resistance, it cannot create any music. An individual aspiring to nirvana—blissful liberation—cannot afford to forget this.

The essence of the Buddha's teachings is encapsulated in *majjhima patipada*—the middle path. If desire, the root cause of all distress and misery is to be conquered, we must lead perfectly balanced lives, avoiding all excess and ensuring that nothing disturbs the tranquility of our mind. The body, according to the Buddhists, must be properly nourished and kept free from painful diseases that can only distract the mind from sadhana (practice). This can only be ensured if the body is healthy and the mind free from fear and other negative emotions like lust, greed, and anger. Emotional disturbances are often caused and always aggravated by inappropriate food. For the Buddhists, food is an integral part of their sadhana. Like right thought and right livelihood, right food can complement and facilitate right contemplation.

This is the foundation of the Buddhist culinary philosophy. Buddhism does not preach denial or forced abstinence. It is true that the monks are expected to lead austere lives but their dietary regimen is not supposed to be followed by the lay.

The Buddhist culinary philosophy is rooted in the teachings of Ayurveda—the ancient Indian science of life. According to Ayurveda, all of us represent a physical and personality type displaying the predominance of a particular *guna* (property). There are three basic properties—*satva, raja,* and *tamas*—that may be roughly translated as tranquil, energetic, and inert. These properties are also discernible in ingredients of food. Another concept that is crucial is of *tridosha*—the three basic impurities—*kapha* (phlegm), *pitta* (bile), and *vata* (nervous energy). These correspond in a loose manner with the elements—earth, fire, and air. These key ideas are also found in the texts of Tibetan medicine and the Chinese yin and yang. In Tibetan medicinal texts, the three *dosha* are referred to as *nyes-pa, rLung, mKhris-pa* and *Bad-kan* corresponding with *vata, pitta,* and *kapha* respectively.

It is not just Ayurveda that has provided the base for Buddhist thinking on food, indigenous traditions and dietary practices in different lands it travelled to have mediated and spurred on its evolution. The inheritance of Buddhist food is truly pan-Asian.

All physical disorders, the Buddhists believe, result from impaired digestion and faulty distribution of nutrients to different vital organs. The cure often entails consumption of special foods to redress the imbalance. Tibetans believe it is essential to make a lifelong commitment to a healthy dietary regime.

The traditional wisdom of Ayurveda and Tibetan and Chinese medicine is not only of therapeutic value. The aesthetic dimension should not be overlooked. The whole approach is holistic. The ecstasy or rapture experienced in samadhi or the flash of illumination that is satori are facilitated by food prepared and imbibed with a sense of purpose and compassion.

The wonderful range that Buddhist repast offers is, to say the least, exhilarating. The Buddha never asked his followers to renounce what was natural and did not interfere with the practice of the middle path. Least dislocation in normal life was caused when one became a Buddhist. A slight adjustment was often enough to 'centre' oneself and regain the lost balance.

It is amazing what joy can be experienced while 'restricting' ones diet to Buddhist menus—even a purely vegetarian one. The colours and textures are seldom interfered with in Chinese and Japanese cooking and the cooking styles can vary from steaming and stir-frying to grilling and baking. The sublime aromatics of Indian cuisine, the chromatic creativity of the Thai, the harmonious fusion of the Sri Lankan and the Indonesians, and the rustic ruggedness of the basic Tibetan diet offer a dazzling range to choose from. From piping hot nourishing soups and crunchy cool exotic salads to *lamay, tempura, momo,* pickles, and relishes to accompany rice or noodles, myriad curries and desserts the Buddhist culinary repertoire is rich and resplendent. There is no risk of oppressive monotony or suffering from a jaded plate. One can easily mix and match, adjusting to the feedback received from the body. The manipulation of the mind through food is most subtly wrought but can be distinctly felt.

Modern researches have validated many of the traditional beliefs about the Buddhist food. An *ahimsak* (purely vegetarian) diet greatly reduces the risk of life-threatening metabolic disorders like cancer, hypertension, diabetes, and chronic heart disease. In many cases, the course of a painful and dangerous disease can even be reversed.

The Buddha realized that no seeker of truth and liberation could continue the arduous journey constantly bothered by pangs of hunger or yearning for pleasant tastes. His holiness the Dalai Lama too has in his lectures repeatedly emphasized that the greatest violence is to go against one's grain or to impose on others an alien way of life. The mind and body are inseparable till one attains liberation or finds illumination. Stirrings of desire can be restrained, if not entirely extinguished, by eating intelligently. Suggestions about Buddhist repast, like all other advice given by the Master, are highly practical. One must find one's own way keeping in mind the basic precepts—*appa deepo bhava* (be your own lamp).

Even non-Buddhists can benefit from adopting and adapting the Buddhists recipes to their requirements. The purity of ingredients, simplicity of cooking styles and opening one's mind to constructive influences and innovations hold the promise for immense benefit for all. The precious essence of Buddhist food can go a long way towards mitigating the sorrows of the body and mind.

Special Ingredients Used

Bamboo Shoots
Tender shoots of the young bamboo are available fresh, or sliced or in cans.

†

Basil
Different types of basil are used in Asian cooking. Two common varieties are holy and sweet basil.

†

Bean Curd
Also known as tofu, is rich in protein. Plain tofu is bland in flavour but absorbs the flavours of the food with which it is cooked. It is also available smoked and marinated.

†

Bean Sprouts
Shoots of the mung bean are readily available. They add the crunch to stir-fries.

†

Chinese Cabbage
Also known as Chinese leaves, has a pale green colour and tightly wrapped head. About two-thirds of the cabbage is stem which has a crunchy texture.

†

Five-Spice Powder
This aromatic powder contains star anise, pepper, fennel, cloves, and cinnamon.

†

Coconut Milk & Cream
Coconut milk should not be confused with coconut water found inside a fresh coconut. The coconut milk used for cooking is obtained from the white flesh of the nut. If left to stand, the thick part of the milk will rise to the surface like cream.

Break open a fresh coconut and remove the brown inner skin from the flesh. Grate the required quantity of flesh and blend with some water in a blender. Strain the mixture through a very fine sieve into a bowl. Stir well before use.

Coconut milk is also available in cans, or in powder form (can be used as a substitute).

†

Dashi
Seaweed flavoured Japanese stock is available in powder form. Diluted vegetable stock may be substituted.

†

Galangal
Fresh galangal tastes and looks a little like ginger. It is also available dried and ground.

†

Hoisin Sauce
A thick, dark brownish-red Japanese sauce that is sweet and spicy.

†

Kaffir Lime Leaves
These impart an aromatic flavour to dishes. The fresh leaves can be frozen for future use.

Lemon Grass

Lemon grass or citronella has a woody texture and a lemony aroma. It is fibrous and always removed before serving.

†

Mirin

A mild, sweet, Japanese rice wine commonly used in cooking.

†

Miso

A fermented bean paste that imparts a rich flavour to Japanese soups.

†

Mooli

This vegetable is a member of the radish family and has a fresh, pungent taste. It has white skin and flesh. When cooked, it should be salted and allowed to drain first, as it has a high water content.

†

Mushrooms

Chinese shiitake mushrooms are used both fresh and dried to add texture and flavour to a dish. All dried mushrooms need to be soaked in warm water for 20-30 minutes before use. Their price may appear exorbitant but remember only a very small quantity is required.

†

Noodles

A great variety of noodles is used in Buddhists recipes. Some commonly used types are:

Cellophane noodles, also known as transparent or glass noodles, are made from ground mung beans.

Egg noodles are made from wheat flour, egg, and water. The dough is flattened and then shredded or extruded through a pasta machine to the required shape and thickness.

Rice noodles are made from ground rice and water. They range in thickness from very thin to wide ribbons and sheets.

Rice vermicelli are thin, brittle noodles that look like strands of hair and are sold in large bundles. They cook almost instantly in hot liquid, provided the noodles are first soaked in warm water. They can also be deep-fried.

Some noodles are delicate, thin, white *Japanese noodles* made from wheat flour in dried form, usually tied in bundles held together with a paper band.

Udon noodles are made of wheat flour and water. They are usually round, but can also be flat.

†

Pakchoi

Also known as bok choi, is a dark green leafy vegetable with long, smooth, white stems.

†

Palm Sugar

Strongly flavoured, hard brown sugar made from the sap of the coconut palm tree. It is available in oriental stores. If you have trouble finding it, use soft dark brown sugar instead.

†

Peanuts

Used for their distinct flavour and their crunchy texture. The skins must be removed before use by rubbing vigorously.

†

Red Bean Paste

A reddish-brown paste made from puréed red beans and crystallized sugar.

†

Rice

Long-grain rice is generally used for savoury dishes. There are many varieties. Long-grained Basmati, which means fragrant in Sanskrit, is generally acknowledged as the best. Thai jasmine rice is also fragrant but is slightly sticky.

†

Rice Vinegar

There are two basic types of rice vinegar: red vinegar is made from fermented rice and has a distinctive dark colour and depth of flavour, and white vinegar is stronger in flavour as it is distilled from rice. If rice vinegar is unavailable, cider vinegar may be substituted.

†

Sake

A strong, powerful, fortified rice wine from Japan.

†

Soy Sauce

A major seasoning ingredient in Asian cooking, this is made from fermented soy beans combined with yeast, salt, and sugar. Chinese soy sauce is of two main types: light and dark. Light soy sauce has a stronger flavour than the sweeter dark sauce, that gives food a rich, red hue.

Vegetable Stock

Take 375 gm / 12½ oz carrots, roughly chopped; 375 gm / 12½ oz turnips, roughly chopped; 650 gm / 1½ lb onions, roughly chopped and 900 gm / 2 lb celery sticks, chopped.

Combine all the ingredients in a large saucepan, simmer uncovered for 1½ hours. Strain through a fine muslin cloth into a bowl and store in a refrigerator till required.

†

Wasabi

A pungent edible root, that is used in Japanese cooking to impart a sharp and a fiery flavour, similar to horseradish. Available fresh and in powder and paste form.

†

Water Chestnuts

Walnut-sized bulbs from an Asian water plant that look like sweet chestnuts. They are sold fresh by some oriental food stores, but are more readily available in cans.

†

Yellow Bean Sauce

A thick paste made from salted, fermented yellow soya beans, blended with flour and sugar.

Light Foods

Buddhism distinguishes, very sensitively, between foods of light and the foods of darkness. The 'light' foods are what the Ayurveda terms *satvik*—essential, pure and easy to digest. Light foods are wonderfully nourishing for the body and mind and help us onwards in our spiritual journey. Grains and legumes, fresh vegetables and fruits, dairy products, nuts and honey are all put in the category of pure foods akin to ambrosia.

Light *satvik* foods are always preferred over the *rajasik* and *tamsik* diet by the seeker. Eating should, as far as possible, be synchronized with the cycle of seasons. *Svabhava* and *prakriti* (natural inclination and temperament and the external milieu) are the key words in this context. It is not very difficult to enjoy a *satvik* Buddhist repast composed entirely of light foods without missing out on flavours. Light foods do not trigger evanescent euphoria but let us experience true ecstasy.

Dark Foods

Dark foods are what the Ayurveda terms *tamasik*—the word derives from *tamas* that means dark. These, the Buddhists believe, dangerously soup up the metabolism, stoke lust and anger, stirring up desire that is the root cause of misery.

Some dark foods are easy to identify like most meats, stale, leftover, oily and excessively spiced food. These foods taint the mind of the diner and can only cause physical discomfort and mental distress.

Tamasik food puts an unnecessary strain on the system as it struggles to digest and excrete the wastes produced. When consumed, such food makes us slothful and prone to doubt and worry. These may be tasty and tempting but at the core remain gross—toxic and intoxicating. The Buddhist masters knew how easy it is to get addicted to junk food. And don't forget, excess is evil. All such edibles that retard our spiritual progress and hinder liberation belong to this list.

Soups & Salads

A wonderful source of nourishment, **soups** are an essential part of many a Buddhist meal. A soup may be thin and clear or have porridge-like consistency. It can tempt the diner with its satin smooth creamy texture or offer a delightful bouquet of crunchy tidbits. It can be an aperitif, a worthy accompaniment or at times a one-dish meal. Quick to prepare, once the stock is ready, a soup can be enjoyed piping hot or refreshingly cold. It lends itself to limitless improvisation, the pool of aromatic liquid holding mirror to changing seasons and reflecting the myriad moods of the contemplating mind.

Salads made with garden fresh greens and other crunchy colourful vegetables are wonderfully refreshing. *Satvik* salads enriched with sprouts, seasonal fruits, and nuts are the epitome of light foods. Preparing and partaking a salad is a joyous celebration of this effort.

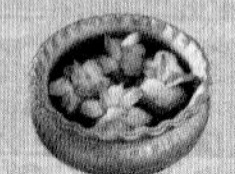

Ochre Invocation

THIS *coconut soup in an earthy hue provides just the right blend of tangy flavours and enticing aroma to embark on an exciting culinary odyssey.*

INGREDIENTS

SERVES 4

Galangal, fresh, peeled, cut into thin slices ~ **5 cm / 2" piece**

Vegetable stock (see p.13) ~ **1 cup / 250 ml / 8 fl oz**

Coconut milk ~ **2 cups / 500 ml / 16 fl oz**

Tofu, cut into thin strips ~ **150 gm / 5 oz**

Red chillies, finely chopped ~ **1-2 tsp**

Light soy sauce ~ **2 tbsp / 30 ml**

Soft brown sugar ~ **1 tsp / 5 gm**

Coriander leaves, fresh, chopped ~ **½ cup / 30 gm / 1 oz**

Salt and black pepper to taste

METHOD

~ Put the galangal, vegetable stock, and coconut milk in a medium-sized pan. Bring to the boil and then simmer, uncovered, over low heat for 8-10 minutes. Stir occasionally.

~ Add tofu strips and red chillies; simmer for another 10 minutes. Stir in the light soy sauce and brown sugar. Add coriander leaves and mix well. Adjust seasoning.

~ Serve immediately, garnished with sprigs of coriander.

The Bhaisajyaguru

The Buddhist believe that all life forms are interrelated. Life is sustained and good health enjoyed by the nourishment provided by food. When we eat, it should be with deep felt gratitude and reverence for what we are imbibing. When we do so we are protected by the Bhaisajyaguru or the Medicine Buddha. This carved panel depicts the Bhaisajyaguru seated in his Paradise protecting all those who practice Buddhist eating.

Veiled Temptation

THIS *Mongolian soup combines a variety of nutrients to present a substantial and tasty one-dish meal. The presentation is innovative. The 'veil' that covers the broth offers a delicious temptation.*

INGREDIENTS

SERVES 4 to 6

Tomatoes, chopped **~ 2 tsp / 10 gm**

Vegetable stock (see p.13)
~ 2 cups / 500 ml / 16 fl oz

Onion, chopped **~ 1 tsp / 5 gm**

Garlic, chopped **~ ½ tsp**

Coriander leaves, fresh, chopped
~ 2½ tbsp / 10 gm

Minced mushroom and tofu
~ 150 gm / 5 oz

Salt **~ 1 tsp / 5 gm**

Ajinomoto **~ ½ tsp**

Refined flour
~ 1½ cups / 200 gm / 6½ oz

Salt and black pepper to taste

METHOD

~ Boil the tomatoes with vegetable stock.

~ Combine onion, garlic, coriander leaves, minced mushroom and tofu, salt, and ajinomoto in a bowl and mix well.

~ Add this mixture to the boiled tomato with vegetable stock and bring to the boil. Gradually, stir in refined flour. Boil for another minute or two. Adjust seasoning.

~ Cover the bowl with a thin layer of dough (that has been kneaded hard, rolled with a pin into a thin sheet).

~ Steam in a steamer for 20 minutes.

~ Serve hot.

Light in Darkness

THIS *dark brown liquid provides the right contrast for the white tofu cubes that float on the surface recalling radiant stars sparkling in the night sky. Invigorating and inspiring.*

INGREDIENTS

SERVES 4 to 6

Shiitake mushrooms, thinly sliced ~ **3-4**

Vegetable stock (see p.13) ~ **5 cups / 1.2 lt**

Miso paste ~ **4 tbsp / 60 gm / 2 oz**

Tofu, cut into bite-sized cubes ~ **150 gm / 5 oz**

Spring onion, washed, sliced ~ **1**

Salt and black pepper to taste

METHOD

~ If using dried mushrooms soak them in hot water for 2-3 minutes. Then drain.

~ Bring the vegetable stock to the boil in a large saucepan. Stir in the miso paste and then the mushrooms; lower heat and simmer for about 5 minutes. Adjust seasoning. Remove.

~ Pour the soups in individual bowls with cubes of tofu. Garnish with spring onion greens.

Food is Ambrosia

Men-Lha is the Medicine Buddha who leads a group of 8 other protective Buddhas in the Buddhist tradition. He is portrayed with a begging bowl filled with nectar, in one hand and the other stretched out in *dan* mudra making the generous gift of good health. The Tibetan Medicine system maintains that most diseases can be cured and illnesses prevented by eating the right food—one that is appropriate to one's physical constitution in temperament. Food, indeed, is ambrosia.

Rainbow Pot

ALL *the goodness of the vegetable kingdom is served in the company of nutritious tofu to present a feast for the eyes. Red and green and shades of yellow all together—a rainbow in a soup bowl.*

INGREDIENTS

SERVES 4 to 6

Smoked or marinated tofu, cubed
~ **200 gm / 6½ oz**

Lettuce, shredded ~ **115 gm / 4 oz**

Groundnut / sunflower oil
~ **2 tbsp / 30 ml**

Spring onions, sliced ~ **3**

Garlic cloves, cut into thin strips ~ **2**

Carrot, thinly sliced ~ **1**

Vegetable stock (see p.13) ~ **4 cups / 1 lt**

Soy sauce ~ **2 tbsp / 30 ml**

Sugar ~ **1 tsp / 5 gm**

Salt and black pepper to taste

METHOD

~ Heat the oil in a pan; stir-fry the tofu cubes until brown. Drain and set aside on absorbent paper.

~ Put the spring onions, garlic, and carrot in the pan and stir-fry for 2 minutes. Add the vegetable stock, and soy sauce.

~ Add sugar, lettuce, and tofu cubes. Heat gently for a minute and adjust seasoning.

~ Serve hot in individual bowls.

Food and the Three Humours

This is a detail from a painting in the Tibetan classic the *Root Treatise* showing the first stem of the allegorical tree that depicts the three humours present in the body. These, when disturbed cause ill-health. The major reason for the distressing imbalance is wrong food. It is imperative that one eats keeping in mind the effect of different seasons on the three humours and the *guna* or the inherent properties of ingredients.

Riches of Poverty

THERE *are times when the pauper can eat like a prince. Shark's fins are an expensive ingredient and also an absolute no-no for the green at heart. This delicacy uses inexpensive substitutes to stunningly replicate the original classic.*

INGREDIENTS

SERVES 4 to 6

Cellophane noodles ~ **150 gm / 5 oz**

Dried Chinese mushrooms ~ **50 gm / 1½ oz**

Bamboo shoots, rinse, slice into thin pieces ~ **115 gm / 4 oz**

Carrots, medium-sized, julienned ~ **2**

Vegetable stock (see p.13) ~ **4 cups / 1 lt**

Vegetable oil ~ **2 tbsp / 30 ml**

Arrowroot powder ~ **1 tbsp / 15 gm**

Water ~ **2 tbsp / 30 ml**

Sesame oil ~ **1 tsp / 5 ml**

Salt and black pepper to taste

Soy sauce ~ **1 tbsp / 15 ml**

Spring onions, finely sliced ~ **2**

METHOD

~ Soak the cellophane noodles in hot water until soft. Drain and cut into small pieces. Keep aside.

~ Soak the mushrooms in warm water for about 30 minutes, drain well, discard stems and slice into thin pieces.

~ Heat the oil in a large saucepan; add mushrooms and stir-fry for about 2 minutes. Add bamboo shoots, carrots, and noodles. Stir vigorously for about 15 seconds. Add vegetable stock. Bring to the boil and simmer for about 15 minutes.

~ Blend arrowroot powder in a little water. Add sesame oil and slowly pour into the soup. Keep stirring to avoid lumps.

~ Season with salt, pepper, and soy sauce. Garnish with spring onion greens and serve hot.

Nirvana in Shades of Green

IF *salads be the food for liberation one need not stray around—this light appetizing salad is the most appropriate diet for the seeker who wishes to travel light.*

METHOD

~ Cook the noodles in boiling water, following the instructions on the packet.

~ Drain the noodles, refresh in cold water, then drain again. Mix the noodles together with all the prepared vegetables.

~ **For the dressing**, combine all the ingredients in a small bowl; then pour into the noodle and vegetable mixture.

~ Toast the sesame seeds and peanuts.

~ Sprinkle the sesame seeds and peanuts evenly over individual salad portions and serve.

INGREDIENTS

SERVES 4

Cellophane noodles ~ **350 gm / 12 oz**

Carrots, julienned ~ **2**

Cucumber, peeled, cut into cubes ~ **½**

Celeriac, peeled ~ **115 gm / 4 oz**

Springs onions, sliced ~ **6**

Water chestnuts, sliced ~ **8**

Bean sprouts, washed, pat dried ~ **175 gm / 6 oz**

Green chillies, fresh, small, deseeded, chopped ~ **175 gm / 6 oz**

For the dressing:

Dark soy sauce ~ **1 tbsp / 15 ml**

Light soy sauce ~ **1 tbsp / 15 ml**

Clear honey ~ **1 tbsp / 15 ml**

Sesame oil ~ **1 tbsp / 15 ml**

Salt and black pepper to taste

For the garnish:

Sesame seeds ~ **2 tbsp / 20 gm**

Peanuts ~ **115 gm / 4 oz**

Roots & Shoots, Seeds & Grains

THIS *salad showcases almost effortlessly the complete life cycle in the plant kingdom. The interdependence between plants and humans is underlined. Partake gratefully.*

INGREDIENTS

SERVES 4 to 6

Bamboo shoots, rinsed, pat dried, sliced into thin pieces ~ **175 gm / 6 oz**

Rice ~ **2 tbsp / 30 gm / 1 oz**

Shallots, rinsed, pat dried, sliced into thin pieces ~ **100 gm / 3¼ oz**

Garlic cloves, crushed ~ **2**

Spring onions, rinsed, pat dried, sliced into thin pieces ~ **100 gm / 3¼ oz**

Juice of lime ~ **1**

Salt to taste

Granulated sugar ~ **1 tsp / 5 gm**

Mint leaves ~ **1 small sprig**

Sesame seeds ~ **1 tsp / 3 gm**

METHOD

~ Sauté the rice in a frying pan till golden brown. Remove and grind to fine crumbs.

~ Mix rice crumbs with shallots, garlic, spring onions, lime juice, salt, granulated sugar, and mint leaves together in a bowl.

~ Add bamboo shoots, toss, sprinkle with sesame seeds and serve.

Essence is Nourishment

The basic purpose of food is to provide nourishment for the body and mind. The supreme goal of a Buddhist's life is to liberate the soul from the bondage of karma. Eating focuses on ensuring essential nourishment. In Tibet the rustic and robust repast comprises a bowl of roasted barley and thick butter-tea. Elsewhere too in the Buddhist world the emphasis is on simplicity and *satvik*—foods that are easy to digest, pure and subtle.

Sweet & Tangy Twins

CARROTS *and radish or daikon are common vegetables and quite unreasonably underestimated. Paired in the salad they show off what they can accomplish balancing each other's strengths and weaknesses.*

INGREDIENTS

SERVES 4

Daikon, thickly peeled, cut lengthways and crossways to make thin matchsticks ~ **2**

Carrots, peeled, cut lengthways and crossways to make thin matchsticks ~ **2**

Salt ~ **1 tbsp**

Caster sugar ~ **3 tbsp / 25 gm**

Rice vinegar ~ **4½ tbsp / 70 ml**

Sesame seeds ~ **1 tbsp / 10 gm**

METHOD

~ Place the daikon and carrot in a mixing bowl. Sprinkle with salt and mix well with your hands. Leave for about 30 minutes. Drain the vegetables in a sieve and gently squeeze out the excess liquid, then transfer them to another mixing bowl.

~ Mix the sugar and rice vinegar together in a bowl. Stir well until the sugar has completely dissolved. Pour over the daikon and carrot and leave for at least a day, mixing well to blend.

~ Put a small heap in a small bowl or a plate. Sprinkle with sesame seeds and serve.

Mudra

Literally a seal or a grain of food—mudra also means stylized gestures of hands and fingers expressing a particular intent. Combined with an appropriate asana it is believed to be an effective aid during the practice of meditation. The Buddhist icons illustrate the major mudras—*abhaydan* (blessing of fearlessness), *bhumi-sparsha* (calling upon the Earth to testify to the Buddha's attainment of Enlightenment) or *dharma chakra pravartana,* setting the wheel of dharma in motion by preaching the first sermon.

Sprouts from the East

SPROUTS *are a popular ingredient in oriental cuisine. Usually it is germinating mung beans that provide the sprouts. This salad looks and tastes very different due to the use of the Brussel sprouts. Extremely satisfying.*

METHOD

~ Heat the oil in a preheated wok or frying pan; add Brussel sprouts and spring onions and stir-fry for 2 minutes, without browning.

~ Stir in the five-spice powder and soy sauce, and cook, stirring, for a further 2-3 minutes. Adjust seasoning.

~ Serve hot, as an accompaniment.

INGREDIENTS

SERVES 4 to 6

Brussel sprouts, washed, pat dried, trimmed, shredded ~ **450 gm / 1 lb**

Sesame or sunflower oil ~ **1 tsp / 5 ml**

Spring onions, sliced ~ **2**

Five-spice powder ~ **½ tsp**

Light soy sauce ~ **1 tbsp / 15 ml**

Salt and black pepper to taste

The Cosmic Sound

Ghanta—the bell—is used with the *vajra* held in the other hand while performing ritual worship. It symbolizes primeval sound and is rung to call the faithful and focus attention on the rite at hand. It also represents supreme knowledge and employment of skilful means to attain liberation.

Snacks & Starters

Light and appetizing, **snacks & starters** are in a Buddhist meal, akin to an invocation. It is the initial step that indicates the direction of a thousand of miles long journey of self-exploration.

These, like the overture in a piece of music, set the tone with initial notes for what is to follow. The recipes are seldom complicated or presentation ostentatious. Effortless elegance is strived at and simplicity is the guiding principle. The palate is gently titillated and an invitation held out to anticipate in a tranquil manner the future course of the culinary journey. These are usually partaken at teatime and often substituted for a main course when one wants not to be burdened with a heavier meal.

Emerald Momos

THE *dumpling comes in many avtars—dim sums and momos being the most popular. The art is to have a thin, translucent casing that encapsulates a filling of the diner's choice—in this case emerald hued spinach blended with tofu.*

INGREDIENTS

SERVES 4 to 6

For the dough:

Refined flour ~ **1¼ cups / 150 gm / 5 oz**

Boiling water ~ **3 tbsp / 45 ml**

Cold water ~ **1½ tbsp / 25 ml**

Vegetable oil ~ **½ tbsp**

For the filling:

Minced fried tofu ~ **75 gm / 2½ oz**

Spinach, boiled, coarsely chopped, mashed ~ **45 gm / 1¼ oz**

Capsicum, chopped ~ **15 gm / ½ oz**

Sesame oil ~ **½ tsp**

Clear honey ~ **1 tsp / 5 ml**

Light soy sauce ~ **½ tbsp**

Cornflour ~ **1 tsp / 5 gm**

Salt and black pepper to taste

METHOD

~ **For the dough**, sift the flour into a bowl, stir in the boiling water, then the cold water and finally, the oil. Mix well and knead until smooth. Divide the dough into 16 equals parts. Shape each into small balls then press flat to give circular shape (you may use a rolling pin if required).

~ **For the filling,** mix together all the ingredients until well blended.

~ Place a little of the filling in the middle of the small disc and bring the edges together pinching them tight to make a little pouch.

~ Line a steamer with a damp towel. Place the dim sums in it and steam for about 10 minutes.

~ Serve with sauces of your choice.

Tempura Nirvikar

DRAPED *in translucent batter this Japanese delicacy is a demonstration of how simplicity can become sublime.* Nirvikar *(blemishless) is the best way to describe it. Ideal for those who wish to keep the mind unwavering.*

INGREDIENTS

SERVES 4

Aubergine (eggplant), sliced into thick slices and halved ~ **½**

Okra, washed, pat dried, trimmed ~ **4**

Baby corns, washed, pat dried, trimmed ~ **4**

For the batter:

Ice-cold water ~ **1 cup / 250 ml / 8 fl oz**

Rice flour ~ **2 tbsp / 30 gm / 1 oz**

Refined plain, sifted, plus extra for dusting ~ **¾ cup / 90 gm / 3 oz**

Salt to taste

Ice cubes ~ **2-3**

Vegetable oil and sesame oil for frying

METHOD

~ Soak the aubergine in cold water until just before frying. Drain and pat dry.

~ **For the batter**, pour the ice-cold water into a mixing bowl, add the rice flour and mix well. Add the flour and salt and very roughly fold in with a fork. Do not beat. The batter should still be quite lumpy. Add the ice cubes.

~ Pour in enough oil to come halfway up the depth of a wok or deep-fryer. Heat the oil till smoking.

~ Lightly dust the vegetables with flour, dip into the batter and mix. Shake off the excess batter and lower the vegetables carefully into the wok. Deep-fry, 2 to 3 pieces at a time, until crisp. Remove and leave to drain on absorbent paper.

~ Serve immediately with soy sauce.

Radiant Repasts

Fruits, milk and nuts are highly valued in Buddhist recipes. These are categorized as light foods—not only easy to digest but also uplifting and accelerating our progress on the spiritual path. Such foods become even more potent when blessed by a holy personage. Touched by the Dalai Lama even simple fare becomes truly radiant.

Sadhak's Satay

SATAY—*Malay-Indonesian seekh kebab—is usually prepared with mini chicken cubes or beef. This vegetarian version renounces all meats and offers a delightful substitute for the* sadhak—*the seeker.*

INGREDIENTS

SERVES 4 to 6

Cottage cheese ~ **250 gm / 8 oz**

Yam, boiled, cubed ~ **100 gm / 3¼ oz**

Capsicum ~ **100 gm / 3¼ oz**

Vegetable oil ~ **3 tbsp / 45 ml**

For the peanut sauce:

Garlic, chopped ~ **1 tbsp / 15 ml**

Onion, small, chopped ~ **1**

Red chillies, crushed, chopped ~ **3-4**

Kaffir lime leaves, torn ~ **3**

Lemon grass stalk, bruised, chopped ~ **1**

Curry paste ~ **1 tsp / 5 gm**

Coconut milk ~ **1 cup / 250 ml / 8 fl oz**

Cinnamon stick ~ **1 cm**

Peanut butter ~ **75 gm / 2½ oz**

Tamarind juice ~ **2 tbsp / 45 ml**

Light soy sauce ~ **2 tbsp / 30 ml**

Dark brown sugar ~ **30 gm / 1 oz**

Juice of lime ~ **½**

METHOD

~ Heat half the oil in a large frying pan. Add the cottage cheese and yam; stir-fry for 3-4 minutes. Add the capsicum in the end and continue to stir-fry for another 45 seconds. If you like you may pierce the ingredients through a skewer and grill.

~ **For the peanut sauce**, heat the remaining oil in a large frying pan; add garlic and onion. Cook for 3-4 minutes, stirring, until the onion is soft.

~ Add the red chillies, kaffir lime leaves, lemon grass, and curry paste. Cook for 2-3 minutes.

~ Stir in the coconut milk, cinnamon stick, peanut butter, tamarind juice, soy sauce, lemon juice, and sugar.

~ Reduce the heat and simmer gently for 15-20 minutes until the sauce thickens, stirring occasionally.

~ Mix the cottage cheese and other vegetables with the prepared sauce.

~ Serve garnished with fresh coriander leaves, sliced red chillies, and spring onions, accompanied by peanut sauce.

Fruity Fritters

THE *apparently simple starter is full of pleasant surprises packing as it does contrasting colours, textures, and flavours. It can be independently savoured or used as an unusual accompaniment.*

INGREDIENTS

SERVES 4 to 6

Bananas, small, peeled ~ **8**

Self-raising flour ~ **115 gm / 4 oz**

Rice flour ~ **40 gm / 1¼ oz**

Salt ~ **½ tsp**

Water ~ **1 cup / 250 ml / 8 fl oz**

Vegetable oil for deep-frying

Sugar to sprinkle

Lime, cut into wedges ~**1**

METHOD

~ Sift both the flours with salt into a bowl. Add just enough water to make a batter of smooth coating consistency. Mix well.

~ Dip the bananas in the batter, ensure that these are well coated.

~ Heat the oil in a pan. Deep-fry the battered bananas until crisp and golden. Remove and drain the excess oil on absorbent paper towels.

~ Sprinkle with sugar and squeeze the lime over the fritters. Serve hot.

The Buddha Turning the Wheel of Dharma

After attaining Enlightenment the Buddha preached his first sermon to five ascetics at Sarnath. This event is known as *dharma chakra pravartana* or turning the Wheel of Dharma and marks an important landmark for the Buddhists. This bronze icon dating back to the Ming period in China shows the Buddha with his hands gesturing the 'turning of the wheel'.

Swad Chakras

THESE *disc-shaped almond enriched savoury corn cakes are an irresistible temptation. They recall the* sansar chakra—*the eternal cycle of birth, death and rebirth caused by karma. Transcend the tasty temptation if you can.*

INGREDIENTS

SERVES 4 to 6

Fresh corn on the cob / canned sweet corn kernels ~ **2 / 350 gm / 12 oz**

Almonds ~ **4**

Garlic clove ~ **1**

Onion, chopped coarsely ~ **1**

Coriander powder ~ **1 tsp / 5 gm**

Vegetable oil ~ **2-3 tbsp / 30-45 ml**

Gram flour ~ **45 gm / 1½ oz**

Coconut, desiccated ~ **2 tbsp / 30 gm / 1 oz**

Spring onions, finely shredded ~ **2**

Celery leaves, finely shredded (optional) ~ **a few**

Salt to taste

METHOD

~ Cook the corn on the cob in boiling water for 7-8 minutes. Drain, cool and, strip the kernels from the cob. If using canned kernels, drain them well.

~ Grind the almonds, garlic, onion, and coriander to a fine paste in a food processor. Heat a little oil and fry the paste until it exudes the typical aroma.

~ Add the aromatic paste to the gram flour and make a batter of coating consistency. Add the coconut, spring onions, celery leaves, and salt.

~ Heat the remaining oil in a shallow-frying pan. Drop large spoonfuls of batter into the pan and cook for 2-3 minutes until golden. Turn the fritters over and cook until golden brown and crispy. Cook in small batches. Serve hot.

Maitreya

Maitreya is the Buddha of future—the final hope of distressed humanity—and associated with the sun God Mitra. He is generally depicted with matted locks sitting in the *lalita* posture. He is believed to be dwelling in the *tushita* heaven. The images of the loving one are often carved out of rock or made with clay and then gilded.

Verdant Flutes

THE *hollow tubes made with delicious green gram paste can hold their own against any other skewer. Steaming of the main ingredient keeps the dish wonderfully light and nutritious without sacrificing taste.*

INGREDIENTS

SERVES 4 to 6

Green gram, fresh ~ **150 gm / 5 oz**

Onions, chopped ~ **30 gm / 1 oz**

Cumin seeds, roasted ~ **1 tsp / 3 gm**

Soy sauce to taste

Salt to taste

Red chilli powder ~ **½ tsp**

Green coriander, chopped ~ **1 tbsp / 4 gm**

Cornflour ~ **1 tbsp / 10 gm**

Vegetable oil for grilling / basting

Juice of lime ~ **1**

METHOD

~ Steam green gram in a bamboo basket till tender and cooked. Remove, mix with the remaining ingredients (except the last three) and blend for 30 seconds till roughly crushed.

~ Add cornflour and knead well into a hard dough. Divide the dough equally and make rolls of about 4" length.

~ Baste the griddle with a little oil and lightly grill the rolls on all sides till done.

~ Serve hot with a dash of lime juice.

Buddha in *Bhumisparsha* Mudra

Prince Siddhartha spent many years in meditation striving to solve the riddle of existence and to liberate himself from the bondage of karma. When the Buddha attained Enlightenment he called Earth as an impartial witness to testify to this event. Touching the ground with hand symbolizes this event. Mother Earth is venerated because it sustains all life and provides food for all her children in diverse forms.

Main Course

It is amazing how a perfectly balanced Buddhist meal can be prepared with inexpensive and easily available ingredients. This does not mean that the Buddhist **main course** is bland or lacks variety. The cooking techniques employed range from steaming, boiling, stir-frying to shallow and deep-frying. The emphasis is on preserving natural textures and flavours as far as possible. Subtle aromatics and imaginative spicing transforms the simplest dishes to something sublime.

The main course, in most Buddhist meals, is composed by combining a vegetable or a melange of vegetables with rice or noodles. The riot of colours, the enticing aromas and fascinating flavours encountered in these recipes are enough to satisfy the most demanding epicure.

Saumya-Sheel

WHAT *can be more gentle than gently stir-fried greens! This main course can be the envy of many a light salad. A perfect repast to cultivate the virtues of* saumya-sheel *(modesty and virtue). Marry it with steamed rice to experience bliss.*

INGREDIENTS

SERVES 4 to 6

Broccoli florets, washed, pat dried
 ~ 225 gm / 7 oz

Sugar snap peas, washed, pat dried
 ~ 115 gm / 4 oz

Bamboo shoots, very thinly sliced
 ~ 150 gm / 5 oz

Chinese cabbage, shredded
 ~ 1 / 250 gm / 8 oz

Spring onions, washed, pat dried **~ 4**

Sunflower oil **~ 3 tbsp / 45 ml**

Sesame oil **~ 1 tbsp / 15 ml**

Garlic clove **~ 1**

Salt and black pepper to taste

Soy sauce **~ 2 tbsp / 30 ml**

Water **~ 2-3 tbsp / 30-45 ml**

Sesame seeds, toasted **~ 1 tbsp / 15 gm**

Bell pepper to garnish

METHOD

~ Heat the sunflower and sesame oils in a preheated wok or a large frying pan; add garlic and stir-fry for 30 seconds.

~ Add broccoli florets and stir-fry for about 3 minutes. Add the sugar snap peas and bamboo shoots; cook for another 2 minutes, then toss in the cabbage and spring onions and stir-fry for a further 2 minutes. Adjust seasoning.

~ Pour in soy sauce and water; stir-fry for a another 3-4 minutes.

~ Sprinkle with toasted sesame seeds and garnish with bell pepper. Serve hot .

Structure of Life

The design of this five-storied *stupa* in Nepal represents *panchmahabhutas* or the five fundamental elements. These elements are also correlated to the colours of the *Dhyani* Buddhas—presiding over different directions and pure geometrical shapes. From ground up the different floors symbolize the earth, water, fire, air and space. According to Ayurveda, and Chinese and Tibetan medicines different ingredients of food correspond to these elements.

Nishkam Shak

THIS *dish is for the days when one feels like practicing austerities and getting back to the basics. Just the cabbage with a hint of chilli and a drop of oil to avoid any stirrings of* kamana *(desire)—a celebration of the* shak *(leafy vegetables).*

INGREDIENTS

SERVES 4 to 6

Cabbage, small, washed, pat dried, shredded ~ **1**

Vegetable oil ~ **1 tbsp / 15 ml**

Black peppercorns ~ **¼ tsp**

Red chillies, fresh, washed, pat dried, deseeded, cut into small pieces ~ **2**

Vinegar ~ **1 tbsp / 15 ml**

Sugar ~ **½ tbsp**

Soy sauce ~ **1 tbsp / 15 ml**

Sesame oil ~ **1 tsp / 5 ml**

Salt to taste

METHOD

~ Heat the oil in a preheated wok until smoking; add black peppercorns and red chillies.

~ Add the cabbage and stir-fry for about 1-2 minutes. Add vinegar, sugar, soy sauce, sesame oil, and salt. Blend well and serve immediately.

The Prayer Wheel

The mantra—*om mane padma hum* (the jewel is in the lotus)—is written on a piece of consecrated paper and placed inside a rotating drum or a miniature barrel. The devout believe that as the devotees turn these prayer wheels clockwise, merit is accrued for recitation and circumbulation.

Prayas: Peppery & Pungent

THE *way to salvation is seldom free from roadblocks. The obstacles have to be removed by conscious effort*—prayas. *At times, to attain purity of body and mind may mean resorting to methods: peppery and pungent!*

INGREDIENTS

SERVES 4 to 6

Walnuts / Pine nuts / Hazel nuts ~ **30 gm / 1 oz**

Vegetable oil ~ **1½ tbsp / 25 ml**

Horseradish, cut into thin strips ~ **115 gm / 4 oz**

Yellow and red bell peppers, cut into bite-sized pieces ~ **115 gm / 4 oz**

Carrots, cut into thin strips ~ **115 gm / 4 oz**

Juice of orange ~ **1**

Coriander leaves, chopped ~ **2 tbsp / 8 gm**

Salt and black pepper to taste

METHOD

~ Toast the nuts in a preheated wok until golden brown. Remove and keep aside.

~ Heat the oil in a wok; when close to smoking, add the vegetables and cook for 2-3 minutes on high heat. Remove and keep aside.

~ Pour the orange juice into another wok and simmer for 2 minutes. Remove and keep warm.

~ Arrange the vegetables attractively on a warmed platter; sprinkle over the coriander leaves and season to taste with salt and black pepper.

~ Drizzle over the orange juice, sprinkle with nuts and serve immediately.

Vajrasatva

The word translates as the 'soul of the *vajra*'—the thunderbolt. *Vajra* also means a diamond, the hardest of all substances and the noblest of all stones. *Vajra* stands for the pure doctrine of dharma that like the illuminating flash of powerful lightening pierces darkness of ignorance or like a diamond cut through the hardest of obstacles. The right food not only fortifies the body but also makes the truth-seeking mind as strong and brilliant as a diamond.

Tri-Ratna Manjusha

THE *three* ratna *(gems) cherished by the Buddhists are the Buddha, the* dhama, *and the* sangha. *This recipe serves as the constant reminder of the* tri-ratna *by putting on the platter a trio of succulent vegetables.*

INGREDIENTS

SERVES 4

Bamboo shoots, sliced ~ **115 gm / 4 oz**

Baby corn cobs, roughly chopped ~ **115 gm / 4 oz**

Broccoli florets ~ **115 gm / 4 oz**

Vegetable oil ~ **4 tbsp / 60 ml**

Salt ~**1 tsp / 5 gm**

Light brown sugar ~ **1 tsp / 5 gm**

Vegetable stock (see p. 13) or water, if necessary ~ **a little**

Light soy sauce ~ **1 tbsp / 15 ml**

METHOD

~ Heat the oil in a preheated wok; stir-fry the vegetables on high heat for about 2 minutes. Add the salt and brown sugar and a little stock or water, if necessary, and continue stirring for another minute.

~ Add the soy sauce. Blend well and serve.

Thangka Painting

These Tibetan Buddhist paintings on a scroll can be rolled up and stored when not on display. The thangkas are of many type but all seek to bridge the gap between the material and the spiritual, real and the fantastic, microcosm and the macrocosm. Food like a thangka plays an important role in mood manipulation and altering the state of our mind. It is essential to follow a suitable dietary regime before embarking on the spiritual mystic path.

Padmabha

PADMA *or the lotus represents the seat of awakened knowledge—the heart. It has reddish hue symbolizing compassion and discriminating deployment of energy. This curried delicacy draws from the Thai Buddhist repertoire.*

INGREDIENTS

SERVES 4 to 6

Tofu, rinsed, cut into small cubes ~ **175 gm / 6 oz**

Red chillies, sliced ~ **3-4**

Coconut milk ~ **2 cups / 500 ml / 16 fl oz**

Red curry paste ~**1 tbsp / 15 gm**

Light soy sauce ~ **3 tbsp / 45 ml**

Palm sugar ~ **2 tsp / 10 gm**

Button mushrooms, washed, pat dried, quartered ~ **250 gm / 8 oz**

Salt and black pepper to taste

Green beans, washed, pat dried, stringed, trimmed ~ **115 gm / 4 oz**

Kaffir lime leaves, torn ~ **4**

Coriander leaves, to garnish

METHOD

~ Heat one third of the coconut milk in a wok or a saucepan until it begins to separate and an oily sheen appears on the saucepan.

~ Now add the red curry paste, soy sauce, and palm sugar. Mix well. Add mushrooms; stir and cook for a minute and a half. Adjust seasoning.

~ Stir in the remaining coconut milk and bring back to the boil. Add the green beans and tofu; simmer gently for about 5 minutes. Bring to the boil again till the gravy is just enough to coat the vegetables.

~ Add kaffir lime leaves and chillies. Garnish with coriander leaves and serve.

Panchamrita

THE *word literally translates as five kinds of nectar and the five lentils that comprise this delicacy are indeed like ambrosia. And, the jewel in the crown is the unusual tempering with sesame seeds.*

INGREDIENTS

SERVES 4 to 6

Bengal gram ~ **100 gm / 3¼ oz**

Black gram, washed ~ **50 gm / 1½ oz**

Split red gram ~ **50 gm / 1½ oz**

Green gram, washed ~ **50 gm / 1½ oz**

Green gram, split ~ **50 gm / 1½ oz**

Onion, sliced ~ **1**

Turmeric powder ~ **½ tsp**

Salt to taste

Lime juice ~ **2 tbsp / 30 ml**

Vegetable oil ~ **5 tsp / 25 ml**

Cumin seeds ~ **1 tsp / 3 gm**

Sesame seeds ~ **1 tsp / 3 gm**

Green chilli, chopped ~ **1 tbsp / 15 gm**

Garlic, chopped ~ **1 tbsp / 15 gm**

Coriander leaves, chopped ~ **1 tsp**

METHOD

~ Wash and soak the dals together for 1 hour. Boil the dals in 4 cups of water with onions and turmeric powder. Boil for about 45 minutes till the dals are semi mashed. Add salt and lemon juice and continue to cook on slow fire.

~ Heat the oil in a frying pan; add the cumin and sesame seeds. Cook for 10 seconds and then add green chilli and garlic. Cook till golden brown and then pour the tempering in the dal mixture.

~ Check the seasoning and then serve hot garnished with coriander leaves.

Beautiful Bitters

THE *bondage of karma ties us down to an existence that is more often than not full of misery. Misery is one of the cardinal truths preached by the Buddha. Liberation comes when we realize this and bitter becomes beautiful.*

INGREDIENTS

SERVES 4 to 6

Bitter gourd, medium-sized, washed ~ **4**

Vegetable oil ~ **4 tbsp / 60 ml**

Garlic cloves, crushed ~ **4**

Onions, chopped ~ **50 gm / 1½ oz**

Tofu, mashed ~ **175 gm / 6 oz**

Capsicum, chopped ~ **1**

Coriander leaves, chopped ~ **1 tbsp / 4 gm**

Curry powder ~ **1 tsp / 5 gm**

Salt to taste

Soy sauce ~ **2 tsp / 10 ml**

METHOD

~ Slit open the bitter gourd lengthwise. Scoop out the seeds and pulp. Rub with salt and put them on a tray. Keep aside.

~ Heat the oil in a frying pan; add garlic and sauté for 30 seconds. Add onion and cook till transparent.

~ Add tofu, capsicum, and coriander leaves. Add curry powder and salt; cook till the moisture is evaporated. Stir in soy sauce and cook for another 30 seconds. Remove and keep aside to cool.

~ Stuff the bitter gourd with the tofu mixture and press gently to ensure that maximum filling goes in without breaking the bitter gourd.

~ Place the stuffed bitter gourds on a greased tray and cook in a preheated oven till done. Serve hot with the leftover stuffing poured over the stuffed bitter gourds.

Miso Flavoured Vegetables

WHAT *sets this dish apart from million other stir-fries is the typical miso flavour. It is a veritable harmony of diverse tints and tastes.*

INGREDIENTS

SERVES 4 to 6

Capsicum, washed, pat dried ~ **1**

Red and yellow pepper, washed, pat dried ~ **1 each**

Baby corns, washed, pat dried ~ **115 gm / 4 oz**

Shiitake mushrooms, washed, pat dried ~ **115 gm / 4 oz**

Carrots, medium, cut into bite-sized pieces ~ **2**

Onion, medium, washed, pat dried ~ **1**

Vegetable oil ~ **2 tbsp / 30 ml**

Miso paste ~ **2 tbsp / 30 gm / 1 oz**

Soy bean paste ~ **2 tbsp / 30 gm / 1 oz**

Salt and black pepper to taste

Sesame seeds, toasted ~ **1 tbsp / 10 gm**

Pickled ginger, thinly sliced ~**1 tbsp**

Spring onions, medium bulbs, chopped ~ **2**

METHOD

~ Heat the oil in a wok; stir-fry the vegetables on high heat for 2 minutes.

~ Add the miso and soy bean pastes and stir for another minute. Adjust seasoning. Remove from flame and garnish with toasted sesame seeds, pickled ginger, and spring onions.

~ Serve immediately.

Blessed Food

The true Buddhist displays great reverence towards food. Items of food, flavourful and fragrant, are offered ritually during worship. Specially prepared delicacies are presented with flowers and fragrance creating a veritable symphony of aromas and colours. Blessed by the Master these are distributed as blessing to other devotees. The Buddhists are adviced to prepare their meals and partake them with a feeling of reverence and share them compassionately.

Roop-Ras Achar

ROOP-RAS *(form and content) confuse us only as long as we view them as a duality. When the veil of maya or ignorance is pierced the essential unity becomes transparent.* Achar *convey this in a piquant manner.*

INGREDIENTS

SERVES 4 to 6

Red chilli, fresh ~ **1**

Onion, medium ~ **1**

Garlic clove ~ **1**

Almonds or cashew nuts ~ **8**

Carrots, medium, chopped ~ **3**

French beans, stringed, trimmed ~ **200 gm / 6½ oz**

Cauliflower, small, cut into florets ~ **1**

Cabbage, cut into small pieces ~ **1 small**

Cucumber, cut into small pieces ~ **1**

Vegetable oil ~ **¼ cup / 60 ml**

White vinegar ~ **2 cups / 500 ml / 16 fl oz**

Water ~ **1 cup / 250 ml / 8 fl oz**

Sugar ~ **30-50 gm / 1-1¾ oz**

Salt to taste

Turmeric powder ~ **1 tsp / 5 gm**

METHOD

~ Blend the chilli, onion, and garlic to a paste with the almonds or cashew nuts.

~ Blanch each vegetable separately in boiling water for a minute, refresh immediately by plunging in ice-cold water. Drain and pat dry.

~ Heat the oil in a pan; stir-fry the spice paste until it releases its aroma. Add vinegar, water, sugar, salt, and turmeric powder. Bring to the boil and simmer for about 15 minutes. Add the vegetables and allow to cook for 5 minutes. The vegetables should not be over cooked and must retain their bites.

Kadhi Kamalini

KADHI *is a popular curry amongst Indian vegetarians and different regions have a local variation. This recipe imaginatively brings together* kamal-nal *(lotus stems) to create a flavourful delicacy.*

INGREDIENTS

SERVES 4 to 6

For the dumplings:

Lotus stems, tender, peeled ~ **100 gm / 3¼ oz**

Cornflour ~ **1 tbsp / 10 gm**

Garlic, chopped ~ **2 tsp / 6 gm**

Ginger, chopped ~ **1 tsp / 5 gm**

Carrots, chopped ~ **60 gm / 2 oz**

Capsicum, chopped ~ **30 gm / 1 oz**

Salt to taste

Vegetable oil for frying

For the sauce:

Butter ~ **2 tsp / 10 gm**

Cumin seeds ~ **1 tsp / 3 gm**

Garlic ~ **1 tsp / 5 gm**

Turmeric powder ~ **1 tsp / 5 gm**

Red chilli powder ~ **1 tsp / 5 gm**

Yoghurt, beaten ~ **2 cups / 450 gm / 1 lb**

Cream ~ **¼ cup / 60 ml**

METHOD

~ **For the dumplings,** boil the lotus stems in sufficient water. When cool, mash well. Mix in the remaining ingredients. Divide the mixture equally and shape each into medium-sized balls.

~ Heat the oil in a frying pan; deep-fry the dumplings, a few at a time, till golden brown. Keep aside.

~ **For the sauce,** heat the butter in a pan; add cumin seeds. When it browns, add garlic and sauté for a few minutes. Add turmeric and red chilli powders; mix well. Add yoghurt immediately and cook on low heat till the yoghurt smell disappears and the sauce is a little thicker. Remove from heat and stir in the cream.

~ Place the dumplings in a bowl and pour the boiling sauce over it. Serve hot.

Piyadassi Purnahara

PIYADASSI *means pleasant to look at and this, indeed, is a dish beautiful without compare. What is more it is* purnahara *(a perfectly balanced meal) combining protein-rich tofu with vegetables providing the bounty of vitamins and roughage.*

INGREDIENTS

SERVES 4

Firm tofu, cubed ~ **275 gm / 9 oz**

Cumin powder ~ **2 tsp / 10 gm**

Paprika ~ **1 tbsp / 10 gm**

Ginger, ground ~ **1 tsp / 5 gm**

Cayenne pepper ~ **a good pinch**

Caster sugar ~ **1 tbsp / 15 gm**

Vegetable oil for frying ~ **¼ cup / 60 ml**

Garlic cloves, crushed ~ **2**

Spring onions, sliced thinly ~ **1 bunch**

Red and yellow bell pepper, deseeded, sliced ~ **1 each**

Brown-cap mushrooms, halved ~ **250 gm / 8 oz**

Courgette, large, sliced ~ **1**

French beans, stringed, cut into large pieces ~ **115 gm / 4 oz**

Walnuts ~ **1 tbsp / 15 gm**

Lime juice ~ **1 tbsp / 15 ml**

Clear honey ~ **1 tbsp / 15 ml**

METHOD

~ Mix together the cumin, paprika, ginger, cayenne pepper, and caster sugar with plenty of seasoning. Coat the tofu with this spice mixture.

~ Heat a little oil in a preheated wok or a large frying pan. Cook the tofu over high heat for 3-4 minutes, turning occasionally. Take care not to break up the tofu too much. Remove with a slotted spoon. Wipe dry the wok or pan with paper towel.

~ Add a little more oil to the wok or frying pan and stir-fry the garlic and spring onions for 3 minutes. Add the remaining vegetables and stir-fry over medium heat for 6 minutes, or until the vegetables begin to soften and turn golden. Season well.

~ Return the tofu to the pan. Add walnuts, lime juice, and honey. Heat and serve.

Noodles & Rice

Rice is the staple in most of Asia and it is synonymous with food. It is the staff of life. Buddhists meals are largely composed with rice or **noodles** made with rice. The varieties of rice are many and so are the many forms it takes. The body in a typical meal comprises steamed rice or noodles and seasonable vegetables, legumes, and tofu.

Cooking rice and noodles presents a daunting challenge to the uninitiated. Each variety requires different quantities of water and cooking time has to be just right for the dish to turn out perfect. Don't let this dither you. There is nothing that cannot be accomplished with a little patience and practice a bit like sadhana!

Maitri-Raag

MAITRI *conveys much more than friendship. It is closer to intense empathy with all sentient beings. This recipe playing the* maitri-*raag is inspired by a popular Thai dish.*

INGREDIENTS

SERVES 4 to 6

Dried rice sticks ~ **250 gm / 8 oz**

Vegetable oil ~ **2 tbsp / 30 ml**

Garlic cloves, finely chopped ~ **3**

Red chillies, chopped ~ **1 tsp**

Tofu, thinly sliced ~ **150 gm / 5 oz**

Water chestnuts, chopped ~ **100 gm / 3¼ oz**

Garlic chives, chopped ~ **75 gm / 2½ oz**

Light soy sauce ~ **2 tbsp / 30 ml**

Lime juice ~ **2 tbsp / 30 ml**

Soft brown sugar ~ **2 tsp**

Salt and black pepper to taste

Bean sprouts, scraggly ends removed ~ **1 cup / 90 gm / 3 oz**

Coriander leaves, fresh ~ **a few sprigs**

Peanuts, roasted, chopped ~ **¼ cup / 30 gm / 1 oz**

METHOD

~ Soak the rice sticks in boiling water for 10 minutes or until they are soft. Drain and set aside.

~ Heat the oil in a large frying pan. When the oil is hot, add garlic, red chillies, and tofu; stir-fry for 2 minutes.

~ Add the water chestnuts and stir-fry for 3 minutes. Add the garlic cloves and drained rice sticks to the pan; cover and cook for another minute.

~ Add the soy sauce, lime juice, and brown sugar; toss well for about a minute. Adjust seasoning. Add the bean sprouts, coriander leaves, and peanuts; serve.

Pravratti-Nivritti

THE *Lion city is renowned for its dynamism. Energy is deployed striking a balance between* pravratti-nivritti *(engagement-detachment). This is what the seeker needs to do to cut through the fetters of karma.*

INGREDIENTS

SERVES 4

Dried Chinese mushrooms ~ **20 gm / ¾ oz**

Fine noodles ~ **225 gm / 7 oz**

Sesame oil ~ **2 tsp / 10 ml**

Groundnut oil ~ **3 tbsp / 45 ml**

Onion, small, chopped ~ **1**

Garlic cloves, crushed ~ **2**

Green chilli, fresh, seeded, thinly sliced ~ **1**

Curry powder ~ **2 tbsp / 20 gm**

Green beans, halved ~ **115 gm / 4 oz**

Chinese cabbage, thinly shredded ~ **115 gm / 4 oz**

Spring onions, sliced ~ **4**

Soy sauce ~ **2 tbsp / 30 ml**

Water chestnuts, cooked, chopped ~ **115 gm / 4 oz**

Salt to taste

METHOD

~ Place the mushrooms in a bowl, cover with warm water and soak for 30 minutes. Drain, reserving 2 tbsp of the soaking water, then slice.

~ Bring a saucepan of salted water to the boil and cook the noodles according to the directions on the packet. Drain, transfer to a bowl and add the sesame oil.

~ Put the groundnut oil in a preheated wok. When it is hot, stir-fry the onion, garlic, and green chilli for about 3 minutes. Stir in the curry powder and cook for another minute. Now, add the mushrooms, green beans, Chinese cabbage, and spring onions. Stir-fry for 3-4 minutes more until the vegetables are just then.

~ Add the noodles, soy sauce, reserved mushroom water, and the water chestnuts. Toss over the heat for 2-3 minutes before serving.

Agni

THE *cuisine of the Szechuan region is well known for its fiery temperament.* Agni *(fire) one of the elements is the supreme purifier that removes all dross and burnishes all that it touches. Remember this while partaking these noodles.*

INGREDIENTS

SERVES 4

Thick noodles ~ **350 gm / 12 oz**

Tofu, cooked ~ **175 gm / 6 oz**

Vegetable oil for deep-frying

Spring onions, finely chopped ~ **4**

Garlic cloves ~ **2**

Coriander leaves, finely chopped ~ **2 tbsp / 8 gm**

Black peppercorns, toasted, ground ~**10**

For the dressing:

Sweet chilli sauce ~ **2 tbsp / 30 ml**

Soy sauce ~ **1 tbsp / 15 ml**

Sesame oil ~ **2 tbsp / 15 ml**

Vegetable stock or water ~ **2 tbsp / 30 ml**

Salt to taste

Cashew nuts, roasted ~ **50 gm / 1½ oz**

METHOD

~ Cook the noodles in a saucepan of boiling water until just tender, following the directions on the packet. Drain, rinse under cold running water and drain again.

~ Heat the oil in a pan; deep-fry the tofu and drain the excess oil on absorbent paper. Then shred it coarsely. Add spring onions, garlic, coriander, and black pepper.

~ **For the dressing**, combine all the ingredients (except the cashew nuts) in a large bowl and whisk briskly.

~ Now add the noodles, shredded tofu and cashew nuts to the dressing, toss gently. Adjust the seasoning and serve at once.

Tilottama

TIL *(sesame seeds) gives this dish its distinct character. It becomes* uttam *(attains nobility) when coupled with honey—an ingredient considered quintessentially pure. Buckwheat noodles become a dazzling exotica.*

METHOD

~ Toast the sesame seeds and grind to a paste.

~ Blend the garlic, sesame paste, sesame oil, soy sauce, rice wine, honey, and five-spice powder with a pinch each of salt and pepper in a blender or food processor until smooth.

~ Cook the noodles in a saucepan of boiling water until just tender, following the directions on the packet. Drain the noodles immediately and transfer them to a bowl. Combine the noodles with the blended ingredients and the vegetables.

~ Mix well and serve.

INGREDIENTS

SERVES 4

Soba or buckwheat noodles **~ 350 gm / 12 oz**

Spring onions, sliced **~ 4**

Bean sprouts, washed, pat-dried **~ 50 gm / 1½ oz**

Cucumber, peeled, cut into matchsticks **~ 7½ cm / 3"**

Garlic cloves, chopped **~ 2**

Sesame paste **~ 2 tbsp / 30 gm / 1 oz**

Sesame oil **~ 1 tbsp / 15 ml**

Soy sauce **~ 2 tbsp / 30 ml**

Rice wine **~ 2 tbsp / 30 ml**

Clear honey **~ 1 tbsp / 15 ml**

Five-spice powder **~ a pinch**

Salt and black pepper to taste

Kshudha-Shanti

THERE *are times when food is perceived as nothing more then sustenance for the body. Quelling the pangs of* kshudha *(hunger) is enough. This recipe is for the days when the mood is predominantly ascetic.*

INGREDIENTS

SERVES 4 to 6

Dried vermicelli ~ **350 gm / 12 oz**

Vegetable oil ~ **2 tbsp / 30 ml**

Spring onions, washed, pat dried, sliced ~ **2 tbsp / 30 gm / 1 oz**

Soy sauce to taste

Salt and black pepper to taste

METHOD

~ Cook the vermicelli in a large saucepan in boiling water following the instruction on the packet. Rinse under cold water and drain thoroughly.

~ Heat the oil in a wok; add the spring onions and stir-fry for 30 seconds. Then add the noodles stirring very gently to separate the delicate strands without breaking them. Reduce the heat and continue frying until the noodles turn golden brown.

~ Add soy sauce, salt and pepper to taste. Serve immediately.

Dhyana-Dhanya

DHYANA *(meditation) plays an important role in Buddhist sadhana. This practice is facilitated by an appropriate diet.* Dhanya *(nourishing grains) of rice prepared with spartan fungi cannot be improved upon for this purpose.*

METHOD

~ Remove and discard the mushroom stalks. Then slice the caps thinly.

~ Heat 1 tbsp oil in the wok; stir-fry the spring onions and garlic for 3-4 minutes until softened but not brown. Transfer to a plate and keep aside.

~ Add capsicum and stir-fry for about 2-3 minutes, then add butter and remaining oil. As the butter begins to sizzle, add mushrooms and stir-fry over moderate heat for 3-4 minutes.

~ Loosen the rice grains then stir in the mushrooms.

~ Heat the rice over moderate heat, stirring all the time to prevent sticking. If the rice appears dry, add a little oil. Stir in the cooked spring onions, garlic, soy sauce, and coriander. Cook for a few more minutes to heat through before serving.

INGREDIENTS

SERVES 4 to 6

Shiitake mushrooms, washed, pat dried **~ 350 gm / 12 oz**

Long-grained rice, cooked **~ 175-225 gm / 6-7 oz**

Vegetable oil **~ 3 tbsp / 45 ml**

Spring onions, sliced **~ 8**

Garlic clove, crushed **~ 1**

Capsicum, deseeded, chopped **~ ½**

Butter **~ 30 gm / 1 oz**

Dark soy sauce **~ 2 tbsp / 30 ml**

Coriander leaves, fresh, chopped **~ 1 tbsp / 4 gm**

Salt to taste

Anna-Ankurit

RICE *for more than half of humanity is synonymous* anna—*life-sustaining foodgrains. In this recipe aromatic rice is served with* ankurit *(sprouted) beans to provide a nutritious yet light meal.*

INGREDIENTS

SERVES 6

Fragrant rice ~ **225 gm / 8 oz**

Sesame oil ~ **2 tbsp / 30 ml**

Lime juice, fresh ~ **2 tbsp / 30 ml**

Red chilli, small, deseeded, chopped ~ **1**

Garlic clove, crushed ~ **1**

Root ginger, grated ~ **2 tsp / 10 gm**

Light soy sauce ~ **2 tbsp / 30 ml**

Clear honey ~ **1 tsp / 5 ml**

Pineapple juice ~ **3 tbsp / 45 ml**

Wine vinegar ~ **1 tbsp / 15 ml**

Spring onions, sliced ~ **2**

Pineapple rings, cut into bite-sized pieces or use canned fruit after draining ~ **1**

Sprouted lentils or bean sprouts, washed, pat-dried ~ **150 gm / 5 oz**

Red pepper, deseeded, chopped ~ **1**

Celery, sliced ~ **1**

Cashew nuts ~ **50 gm / 1½ oz**

Sesame seeds, toasted ~ **2 tbsp / 20 gm**

METHOD

~ Soak the rice for about 30 minutes, then rinse in several changes of water. Drain and boil in salted water for 10 minutes. Drain and keep aside.

~ Whisk together sesame oil, lime juice, red chilli, garlic, ginger, soy sauce, honey, pineapple juice, and wine vinegar in a large bowl. Slowly add the rice and stir well.

~ Heat a little oil in the wok spreading a thin film on its surface. Add the spring onions, pineapple rings, sprouted lentils or bean sprouts, red pepper, celery, cashew nut, and sesame seeds; stir briskly to blend. This dish can be enjoyed warm or lightly cold.

Desserts

Desserts should not be confused with sinful indulgence as sweets are included in ritual offerings and are partaken on festive celebrations. Sweet is one of the basic tastes and its well known sugars provide the energy for all that we do. Sweet is synonymous with all pleasant sensations—a sweet smile, a sweet voice, and a sweet smell. In India sweets are shared on all festive occasions usually not as dessert but independently. Most Indian deserts are milk based but elsewhere in Asia, Buddhists prefer to use fresh and candied fruits, jellies and frozen tea. The emphasis once again is on palate cleansing and refreshing lightness.

Tejomay

FRUITS *and nuts are considered the light foods—best source of nourishment that purify the system and hone discriminating intelligence. This dessert is truly* tejomay *(incandescent).*

INGREDIENTS

SERVES 4 to 6

For the almond jelly:

Milk ~ **1 cup / 250 ml / 8 fl oz**

Sugar ~ **75 gm / 2½ oz**

Agar-agar ~ **1 tbsp**

Almond essence ~ **½ tbsp**

Kiwi, medium ~ **1**

Papaya ~ **30 gm / 1 oz**

Watermelon ~ **30 gm / 1 oz**

Strawberries ~ **3-4**

Sugar syrup ~ **½ cup / 125 ml / 4 fl oz**

METHOD

~ **For the almond jelly**, boil the milk with sugar and set aside to cool.

~ Mix agar-agar with lukewarm water and stir into the milk.

~ Add the almond essence and place the mixture to set in the deep freezer. Remove when set.

~ Cut all the fruits and the set almond jelly into small pieces in desired shapes.

~ Pour the sugar syrup over the cut fruits.

~ Serve cold, garnished with blades of lemon grass or any colourful flower.

Mandala

Mandala defines mystic space charged with psychic energies. One who enters the enclosure is protected from assaults of evil forces and finds a sanctuary for meditation. This scroll represents the *Maha-karuna-gardha mandala*—the enclosure of compassionate womb—and is from a Japanese monastery in Kyoto. Tradition maintains that it was transmitted to Japan from China in the ninth century.

Sheetal-Kalash

THE *cool pitcher—that is what the name means—is a mildly sweet dessert and an exceptional coolant. The ingredients used have* guna *(inherent properties) to sooth singed palates and bring down the temper.*

INGREDIENTS

SERVES 4 to 6

Sago, soaked in 3 cups water for 1 hour **~ 1 cup / 200 gm / 6½ oz**

Water **~ 3 cups / 750 ml / 32 fl oz**

Soft brown sugar **~ 1 cup / 200 gm / 6½ oz**

Extra water **~ 1 cup / 250 ml / 8 fl oz**

Coconut milk, well chilled **~ 1 cup / 250 ml / 8 fl oz**

METHOD

~ Pour the sago with the water into a medium-sized pan. Add 2 tbsp brown sugar and bring to the boil over low heat, stirring constantly. Reduce heat and simmer, stirring occasionally, for about 10 minutes. Cover and cook over low heat, stirring occasionally for 2-3 minutes, until the mixture becomes thick and sago grains are translucent.

~ Refrigerate the sago mixture to set.

~ Combine the remaining brown sugar with the extra water in a small pan and cook over low heat, stirring constantly, until the sugar dissolves. Simmer for about 5-7 minutes, until the syrup thickens. Remove from the heat and cool.

~ To serve, put in coconut shells and top with a little sugar syrup and coconut cream.

Anand

ANAND *(joy) is hard to attain in everyday life but in the culinary realm one often comes close. This simple sweet dish is nourishing and satisfying without unnecessary frills.*

INGREDIENTS

SERVES 4 to 6

White or black glutinous (sticky) rice ~ **175 gm / 6 oz**

Soft light brown sugar ~ **2 tbsp / 24 gm**

Coconut milk ~ **2 cups / 500 ml / 16 fl oz**

Water ~ **1 cup / 250 ml / 8 fl oz**

Banana (slightly over ripe), peeled, mashed ~ **2**

Granulated sugar ~ **2 tbsp / 25 gm**

METHOD

~ Combine the rice, brown sugar, half the coconut milk and the water in a saucepan.

~ Bring to the boil and simmer, stirring a little, for about 20 minutes until the rice has absorbed most of the liquid. Preheat the oven to 150°C / 300°F.

~ Moisten the banana with a little milk and mix with the remaining coconut milk, and sugar in a bowl.

~ Put the rice mixture into a large ovenproof dish. Strain and pour the banana mixture evenly over the par-cooked rice.

~ Place the dish in a baking tin. Pour in enough boiling water to come halfway up the sides of the dish.

~ Cover the dish with a piece of foil and bake in the oven until the custard is set. Serve warm or cold.

Kheer

THIS *is the mother of all Indian desserts and occupies a special place in the repertoire of Buddhist recipes. The Buddha broke his famous fast with a bowlful of* kheer *brought to him by the young maiden, Sujata.*

METHOD

~ Soak the rice in water for half an hour.

~ Boil the milk in a thick-bottomed pan, stirring constantly, till it is reduced to $^1/_3$.

~ Add rice to the reduced milk and simmer for 7-8 minutes. Mix in the sugar.

~ Remove the cardamom seeds from the pod and grind coarsely. Sprinkle over the milk mixture.

~ Soak the saffron strands in 1 tsp rose water or lukewarm milk. Crush in a pestle and sprinkle over the *kheer*.

~ Garnish with almond and pistachio slivers and raisins, if desired.

INGREDIENTS

SERVES 4 to 6

Rice picked, washed, drained ~ **100 gm / 3¼ oz**

Milk ~ **4 cups / 1 lt**

Sugar ~ **175 gm / 6 oz**

Green cardamom ~ **6**

Saffron ~ **a few strands**

Rose water ~ **1 tsp / 5 ml**

Almond and pistachios, slivered ~ **6**

Raisins ~ **1 tbsp / 10 gm**

Maya-Moha

MAYA *(illusion) born of ignorance is what keeps us entangled in knots of* moha *(attachment). The ties of acquired taste are not easy to get rid off. Sweet and strong is the temptation of this dessert.*

INGREDIENTS

SERVES 4 to 6

Kabocha pumpkin, washed, peeled, deseeded, cut into 5 cm long and 2 cm thick pieces ~ **1 kg / 2¼ lb**

Coconut milk ~ **3 cups / 750 ml / 32 fl oz**

Granulated sugar ~ **175 gm / 6 oz**

Sal ~ **a pinch**

Pumpkin seed kernels, toasted ~ **a few**

Mint sprigs to garnish ~ **a few**

METHOD

~ Bring the coconut milk to the boil in a saucepan. Add sugar and salt.

~ Add the pumpkin and simmer for about 10-15 minutes until the pumpkin is tender. Decorate each serving with a mint sprig and a few toasted pumpkin seed kernels.

~ Serve warm.

The Rosary

The rosary of beads is one of the main accessories of the Buddhist monks. It is composed usually of 108 *rudraksha* seeds and helps to keep count the number of times a mantra has been recited. Manipulation of the beads is often effortlessly coupled with hand gestures—mudra and mala—performing a choreographed duet so to speak, assisting the seeker to raise the level of psychic consciousness during worship.

Trishna

Trishna *(desire) according to Buddhist belief is the root of all misery. The thirst for pleasure is insatiable. This heavenly dessert makes you yearn for more. Watch out!*

INGREDIENTS

SERVES 4

Vanilla ice cream
~ 2 cups / 500 ml / 16 fl oz

Green tea leaves, dried, powdered
~ 1 tbsp / 15 gm

Lukewarm water from the kettle
~ 1 tbsp / 15 ml

METHOD

~ Soften the ice cream by removing it from the freezer. Do not allow it to melt. Mix the green tea leaves powder and lukewarm water in a cup and make a smooth paste.

~ Put half the ice cream into a mixing bowl. Add the green tea leaves paste with residue liquid and mix well to incorporate. Mix with the rest of the ice cream. Put the treated ice cream back into the freezer.

~ The ice cream is ready to serve after an hour.

Hallowed Offering

Sujata, a young maiden, brought a bowlful of *kheer* to Prince Siddhartha as he sat under the Bodhi tree practicing austerities. After the young ascetic attained Enlightenment and became the Enlightened One he broke his fast with a small mouthful of this offering. Pure and nourishing, the *kheer* is quintessential *naivedya* (offering) and *prasad* (blessed food).

Index

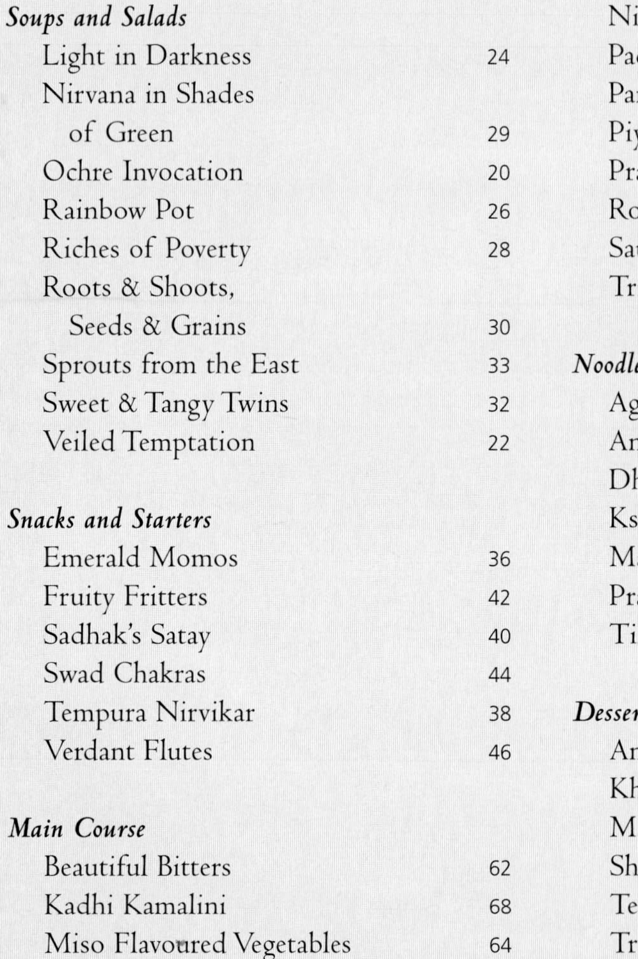